Educating Youths about Stocks: Basics of Buying Stocks

By: Allen Thomas

Copyrights 2013, 2017, 2020 Allen Thomas

First Edition 2013

Revised Edition 2017

2nd Revised Edition 2020

3rd Revised Edition August 2020

Author Of:

The Vessel: You Are More Than You Think, All It Takes Is Faith &

Bro'man's Handbook: Minority Athlete's Guide To Surviving
The Crazy World Of Professional Sports

DEDICATION

TO MY NEPHEW WHO UNWITTINGLY INSPIRED ME TO
WRITE THIS BOOK

INTRODUCTION

Information is power, but so is money. If you use information wisely and money prudently you put yourself in a greater position to succeed financially. Bad information often leads to poor financial decisions. Most people go to work and make their boss rich, but wise people use the money that they earn to make them financially secure.

One way that you can make the money that you earn work for you is to invest it in other people or in the stock market. What do I mean by investing in people? I mean investing in people's dreams and aspirations by loaning them money to start their own business. Someone who starts his or her own business is called an entrepreneur. Someone who loans money to entrepreneurs is referred to as an investor.

There are inherent risks associated with being an entrepreneur and an investor. Specifically, each risks losing their money if the business does not succeed. The same risks apply when investing in the stock market. If the business that you own stock in fails then that company's stock becomes worthless. That's why it is imperative that you thoroughly learn as much as you can about any company that you are interested in investing in. The same holds true regarding a business that your family or friend wants to start. Learning all that you can about a business before investing in it is called performing your "due diligence." You wouldn't go outside in a thunderstorm without a raincoat or an umbrella so why would you invest in someone or in a company before performing your due diligence.

What will you gain from reading this book, well insight about entrepreneurship and how investors play a major role in the success of entrepreneurs? Later in the book you will follow the journey of a local baker looking to grow his business and learn how the decisions that he make could contribute to the success or failure of his business.

First, let me tell you the story that inspired me to write this book. Over a decade ago during the holiday season my sister called to tell me that my then eleven-year-old nephew wanted to buy some stock in *Toys "R" Us*, which has since filed for bankruptcy. Of course, I inquired why and she told me that he had noticed the crowds getting larger each time that they had visited that store. He surmised that the crowd size signaled that *Toys "R" Us* was making a lot of money, which would translate into huge profits. For me, it was refreshing to hear that someone his age was able to grasp the concept of corporate finance albeit in a very fundamental manner.

His interest in purchasing stock in *Toys "R" Us* moved me to search for reading material that would give him more insight about stocks and the stock market. Unfortunately, most of the reading material that I was able to locate were technical in nature and assumed that the reader had more than a basic understanding about investing and entrepreneurship. I wanted to give my nephew with as much information as I could find to foster his interest on that topic, but not overwhelm him with technical information.

Personally, I learned about investing in the stock market from my 7th grade social studies teacher. Go figure, learning about the stock market between history and government lessons, but not in math class. I suspect that my Social Studies' teacher, whose name escapes me, had an affinity for the subject and wanted to share his love of finance with his students.

I believe that my nephew caught the investing bug by listening in on "grown folks' conversations" like all kids do at that age. Between my sister's jokes about my addiction to traveling and how stocks was funding it there is no doubt in my mind that he believed investing in the stock market had a huge plus side. In that context, all kids should do more listening and less playing with electronic gadgets.

After not being able to find reading material that would give my nephew a basic understanding of the stock market and of entrepreneurship, I decided to write him one myself.

This book has been a labor of love. Between work and personal obligations, completing this book has been a challenging feat. I believe that this book encompasses what I had hoped to have purchase for my nephew because I believe that financial literacy is just as important as teaching your child how to drive a car before he or she leaves your home. The earlier a child learns about entrepreneurship and investing the more aware he or she will be in securing their financial future.

Such knowledge may help them comprehend financial products such as 401Ks, mutual funds and other financial products that are put before them when they begin their professional careers either as a blue collar or white collar worker. After reading this book it is my deepest desire that you and your child will find finance interesting enough to seek more literature on the topic. If you do then I believe that you and your child will be in a better position to appreciate and comprehend the information that is contained in more advanced books discussing investing and entrepreneurship.

My experience with investing in the stock market is limited to my own personal experiences trading stocks (buying/selling) as a hobby. Therefore, I encourage anyone reading this book to consult with a financial advisor before engaging in the act of trading stocks. This book is intended to highlight some of the most basic factors to consider before trading stocks or investing in people and is based solely upon my personal opinions and not as a professional financial counselor or stock trader, which I am not.

Trading stocks is very risky and can lead to you losing the money that you had invested, so please don't take trading stocks lightly. Remember, it is ultimately your decision to buy or sell stocks and no one else's. The benefits and rewards of trading stock and investing in people's dreams and aspirations can be exciting, but doing so can also be devastating to your financial security so take it seriously. Performing your due diligence doesn't guarantee success, but it will assist you in making informed decisions regarding a potential investment in any business.

What's A Stock And Why Does It Matter If You Own It

A stock is a financial instrument, which gives you an ownership interest in a company. It is also referred to as a share because you share ownership in that company with other people who had also purchased stock in that same company. Generally, a company's stock is bought and or sold through a financial service company like a bank or a stock brokerage company. Those purchases and sales are generally processed electronically through what is called a stock exchange, which I will discuss in greater detail later in this book.

When people buy stock in a company through a financial service company they are generally not given a certificate of ownership, rather they are given a statement that details their stock purchase. Some of those details generally include the date that the stock was purchased, the price that you paid for that stock and the number of shares that you purchased at that time. People who purchase stock in companies are commonly referred to as a stockholder or a shareholder. Anyone who purchases stock in a company is strongly encouraged to keep the statements that they receive from their financial service company in a safe place. Those statements will be helpful to have when it's time to sell your shares of stock in a company. Although most financial service companies have that information available for their customers online, it is still a good practice to keep a paper copy of your stock purchases in a safe place.

Now, let's look at how important it is for a stockholder to keep track of how much he or she paid for a particular stock. Lets say three years ago you paid $5.00 per share for AWESOME COMPANY's stock and that you bought 100 shares of AWESOME COMPANY's stock at that time. The total price of your stock purchase would have been $500.00. Now, let's say today that AWESOME COMPANY's stock increased in value and is now worth $8.00 per share. If you decide to sell the 100 shares that you own at the current price of $8.00 you would realize a profit of $300.00, which is the difference between what you had paid for that stock 3 years ago and what it's worth today. A financial service company may charge you a fee to sell that stock for you, which will decrease the amount of money that you will receive from the sell of that stock. Also, most times a shareholder will be charged a fee each time that he or she buys a stock so keep that in mind when you calculate the potential cost of purchasing or selling shares of stock. The fees are generally assessed on the total purchase or sale price of the transaction and not on the number of shares involved.

As I said earlier, it's always good to keep track of what you paid for a company's stock so that you will know when it has increased in value. You surely don't want to miss out on an opportunity to make a profit or an opportunity to cut your losses if the price of that stock begins to tank. There are all kinds of Apps that will allow you to track the stock price of a company's stock so I strongly recommend that you download one. In addition, most financial service companies allow their customers to track stocks using their App or website so I encourage you to download their app and utilize your financial service company's website. Most of those websites have tools that you can use to research a company that you own stock in or that you are interested in investing in. I'll talk more about what to research later in this book.

You may be wondering what would make the price of a company's stock tank, well here's an example. Let's say that you own 100 shares of AWESOME COMPANY's stock and that you bought the stock at $5.00 per share, which totals $500. Lets also say that 3 years later you and others who own stock in that company learned that AWESOME COMPANY had been selling inferior products that made people sick. Lets say that the day before that news came out AWESOME COMPANY's stock price was priced at $8.00 per share. Now, lets say when the news about the company's dirty deed got out that its stock price dropped to $4.00 per share. Negative news is one of the major reasons why a company's stock will tank and generally when that happens stockholders rush to sell their interest in that company before the stock price drops even further. If you sold your interest in AWESOME COMPANY at $4.00 per share you would only receive $400 [100 shares x $4.00] minus any fees that your financial service company may charge you for that transaction. Since you paid $5.00 per share and sold the stock at $4.00 per share you would have lost $1.00 per share, which means that you would have lost a total of $100 [$500 - $400 = $100.] One reminder, you only lose money when you sell. If you believe that the company may bounce back then you may want to hold on to that company's stock and ride out the storm, but keep in mind that you will be doing so at your own risk!

Heck, if you have a good and solid reason for holding on to that stock, which is based upon your due diligence you may want to buy more of that stock at the cheaper price. As you can see the decision to sell a company's stock when the price starts to drop is a difficult one especially if the reason for the dip is not related to anything that the company did. In our example, the reason that the company's stock price dropped was based solely upon the action of that company. An event that has nothing to do with a company's action, but results in a dip in its stock price is a downturn in the economy. When people are laid off of their jobs they may not be able to buy a company's products. Most people with little savings are not going to buy high priced electronics, expensive shoes or clothes or travel when they have food to purchase for their families and rent to pay.

Natural disasters such as floods and earthquakes are more reasons why a company's stock price might drop. If the company's factory is permanently destroyed or temporarily closed for an extended period of time because either of those events keep it from making the products that it needs to stay in business then that company may be forced to go out of business. If a company can't make products then it can't make money selling them.

When you purchase stock in a company you are buying an interest in that company. Anyone who owns stock in a company is an investor because their stock purchase is an investment in that company. A person's investment in a company allows that company to do things that it needs to do to grow or sustain the company, such as buying new equipment or hiring more people to make its products. Sometimes companies give their employees an interest in the company in hopes that it will motivate them into working harder or becoming more creative in an effort to grow the company and make it more profitable.

Giving employees stock in a company may not be a bad idea if the employees are making the company a lot of money and I mean a whole lot of it! In 2016, Fortune Magazine reported that the clothing store "Nordstrom" offered its top selling salespeople stock options as a way of rewarding them for their sales effort. Let's say for example that on June 16, 2017, Amazon and Google gave stock options to their employees as an incentive to encourage them to be more creative. I'm not sure if they did or currently do and am only using them in this example because they are recognizable company names. The stock price of Amazon's stock on that date was approximately $987 and the price of Google's stock on that same date was approximately $939. If you sold 100 shares of Amazon stock on that date you would have made a gross profit of $98,700. By the way, on August 21,2020 the price of Amazon stock was approximately $3314 and the price of Google's stock, now called Alphabet, Inc. was approximately $1591. When choosing to invest in a company you should research whether a company offers its employees stock options and research whether doing so affects that company's level of profitability. If it does not then you may want to include that information on your due diligence checklist. Without creative and hard working employees a company won't succeed. Employees and creativity are the engines that allow companies to surpass their competition. Amazon and Google are two companies that have surpassed their respective competition and are leaders in their respective industries. I'm sure that they didn't get that label without creative employees. So look for go-getter companies to invest in.

Why Do Companies Sell Stock

When a company begins to experience growth it should take that opportunity to expand, which may require lots of money to accomplish. If the company's owner doesn't have the money or only has part of it to grow his or her business then they must look elsewhere for it. Thus, the need for investors. One way to attract investors to a company is to offer stock in that company.

Offering stock in the company is a common way businesses raise the money that is needed to produce their products or offer its services. Some of those necessities may include hiring new employees; buying updated factory equipment, office computers, delivery trucks or possibly building or buying a larger facility to produce their products. If an owner of a company can't meet the increase demand for his or her product or service then current and potential customers will go elsewhere for something similar.

Another reason that a company's owner might offer stock in his or her company is to help them pay for the cost to operate their business. One such cost may include the purchase of supplies and material to make the product that they are selling.

The success of a company depends on the decisions that a business owner makes, which can be challenging at times. Wise business owners hire managers to help them run their company so that they don't have to do everything themselves, which makes it easier for them to stay focus on the growth of their business. I can't say this enough, when a company is growing and its owner doesn't make the best decisions regarding the future or survival of his or her company those bad decisions not only affect their business, but they also affects their employees. I will discuss more of that later in this book.

Although increased sales can mean increased profits it doesn't always mean a huge payday for the business owner. Profit is what's left over after a company pays all of its expenses. So if a business owner has a lot of expenses then he or she may not have a lot of money available to expand as quickly as he or she would like to. Such a scenario may lead to the company's owner offering shares of stock in his or her company to help them stay in business. No one starts a business to break even year over year eventually the entrepreneur will want to make a profit and grow his or her company.

Sometimes company owners use the money that they raise from the sell of their company's stock to buy other companies. In 2012, Facebook offered stock to potential investors and raised approximately $16 billion dollars. I'm sure that a company like Facebook doesn't want another social media company coming in and taking some of its business and maybe that's why it purchased "Instagram" and "Face.com" that same year. They may have also purchased those companies to create better user experiences on their platform. Either way, the purchases seemed to be wise and prudent. On August 21, 2020, Facebook's stock price was approximately $270, which is substantially higher than the $38 price that was initially offered for that stock in May 2012. Facebook also purchased FriendFeed in 2009 and "WhatsApp" in 2014. Again, not bad uses of the company's profits.

It is very important for companies like Facebook, Amazon and Google to make good business decisions in order to fend off competitors and to stay relevant and profitable. As I discussed earlier, one way that companies accomplish this is by purchasing their competitors or companies that may add value to their own companies. All of which require lots of money. Not all owners who sell stock in their companies will have the level of success that Facebook's owners had when they raised $16 billion selling stock in their company, but some level of success can be achieved if the company's owner can demonstrate to investors that he or she manages their company well and that their business has a very real chance of being profitable.

Stockholders' Rights

As you have read earlier in this book, when owners of a company make the decision to sell shares of its stock to potential investors it is a major decision. Why, because they are asking those investors to take a chance on them and their company and as a result they become accountable to those investors. Remember, investors have an ownership interest in the company that they invest in and as a result have a right to know how that company is being operated and managed. A poorly managed company may lead to an investor losing the money that he had invested in that company.

As an investor/stockholder/shareholder of a company you have the right to attend stockholder meetings where you can hear directly from the company's executives about how well or how poorly the company is doing. If they are reporting that the company is losing money than those same individuals should also tell the stockholders how they plan to make the company profitable.

During those meetings stockholders may be given an opportunity to vote on business ideas that the owner or top managers of the company may want to implement or pursue. Stockholders may also be given an opportunity to vote on new leadership for the company and should exercise their right to weigh in on that because it's their money that is sustaining that company.

Some of the other issues that may could come up during the stockholders' meeting are lawsuits, which may have been filed against the company. Money to fight the lawsuit or settle a lawsuit will have to be paid out of the company's earnings. Once a company knows that it is or will be facing a lawsuit it usually set aside money that it earned to help pay for the lawyers to fight the lawsuit or use to settle the lawsuit. Setting aside money to fight or settle lawsuits means that those earnings can't be used to grow or expand the company.

Owners and top managers should also use stockholder meetings to reveal or discuss how new laws may impact the company's earnings. One such law may be the raising of the minimum wage that companies are to pay its employees. The additional money that is paid to a company's employees will increase that company's expenses, which will have an impact on that company's profits. Generally, when a company is faced with new laws that will increase its expenses the company passes that additional expense on to its customers in the form of higher prices. Sometimes that option is not always available for one reason or another, which may require the company's owner or its top managers to look elsewhere for the money to pay for the added expenses. At all times the main goal of any business owner is to make money for himself or herself and for the people who invested in their company. Oftentimes the employees are the ones who are drastically affected by the increased costs facing a company in the form of layoffs or a decline of hours worked.

Prior to a stockholders' meeting the company generally sends its stockholders a document concerning important matters that will be brought up during the stockholders' meeting. That document is called a Proxy Statement. That statement makes the stockholder aware of the issues that he/she may be asked to consider and vote on during that meeting.

It is very important for investors/stockholders/shareholders to remember that owners and top managers of the companies that they have invested in have a duty and a responsibility to be truthful and honest with them when making statements about the financial condition of the company. Also, if an owner or top managers of a company fails to manage the company responsibly or presents false or misleading information about the company then the stockholders can sue them.

Stock Buy Backs

After years of having to disclose the company's financial condition to its stockholders or having to get stockholders' approval on certain business matters a business owner or a company's top managers may decide that they no longer want to do that anymore. In such a case they may pursue a stock buyback.

A stock buyback may consist of a business owner or the company's top managers using company funds to buy back most if not all of the company's stock that is owned by their stockholders. If an owner or top managers of a company discovers that there is not enough money in the company's bank account to buy back the company's stock then they may have to borrow the money to do so. In making the decision to repurchase the company's stock the business owner or the top managers of a company must weigh the cost of repurchasing their company's stock against the benefit that they hope to achieve in doing so. Using profits earned or getting a loan to buy back stock will deplete the amount of money that a company has available to grow or expand its business.

Another reason that an owner or top managers of a company may want to buy back their company's stock is to keep another company from taking control over their company. One way that a company can take over a rival's company is to buy most of that rival's company stock to obtain a majority ownership interest in that company. The reasons why a company may want to takeover a rival's company are many, but a major one is to keep that rival from competing against it. Another reason that a company may want to purchase another may be to incorporate some or all of that company's products or services into its own business like what Facebook may have done when it purchased Instagram. Instagram's photo sharing capability has been quite profitable for Facebook. Apple may have used the same rationale when it purchased Beats Electronic, which included Beats streaming service. Publicly traded companies, those that are listed on a stock exchange must continually seek ways to make their investors money otherwise they may lose them to other companies.

There is an old saying often referred to as the Golden Rule, it is as follows: whoever has the gold makes the rules. If an owner or the top managers of a company don't make good business decisions and fail to make their investors money (gold) then they should no longer be entitled to make decision (rules) that affect that company. When profits begin to drop the investors of that company will demand that those individuals be replaced with someone who has a better plan to make the company more profitable. One thing to keep in mind is this: as long as there are stockholders in a company the business owner or top managers of that company will always be accountable to them. As you can see the selling of company's stock may solve a short-term money deficit, but it will come with accountability to the very people who invests in that company.

Stock Exchanges

A stock exchange is just what the name states; it is a mechanism where stocks are bought and sold in exchange for money. Most countries have at least one of them. Before a company's stock is allowed to be listed on a stock exchange the owner or top managers of the company must first get approval from that stock exchange. Moreover, before a company's stock is allowed to be listed it must prepare a prospectus for potential investors disclosing the purpose of the listing, goals the company attempts to achieve with the money raised, the products/services that it will be selling, potential risks or issues that may affect an investor's decision to buy stock in the company coupled with information about who will be leading the company.

All of that information is important to potential investors so that they can make an informed decision about investing in their company. An owner or top manager of a company who does not disclose that kind of information to potential investors or cheat their investors out of their money may find themselves being sued by those same investors or imprisoned. As you can see business owners and top managers must be good and honest stewards of their investors' money otherwise they can face real life consequences.

The two most popular stock exchanges in the United States are the New York Stock Exchange (NYSE) and the NASDAQ, formerly known as the National Association of Securities Dealers Automated Quotations. Like other stock exchanges in the world those two exchanges have their own procedures regarding how a company's stock gets listed on its exchange. Company owners or top managers who want their stock to be listed on a stock exchange often hire lawyers who have the expertise to ensure that those procedures are followed correctly so that their company's stock can be traded without any issues. It takes a lot of time and effort for a company to have its stock listed on a stock exchange, which is good for investors because it allows an investor to get important information about the company in order to make an informed decision before investing in that company.

A company's lawyer must also ensure that the owner or top managers of a company files the appropriate documents with the Securities and Exchange Commission (SEC), which oversees stock exchanges and the companies that are listed on them. The SEC also ensures that any company that is listed on a stock exchange in the United States follow its rules, such as providing its stockholders with information about how well or how poorly its business is doing.

Once you have identified a company that you would like to invest in you should check the NYSE or NASDAQ to see if that company's stock is available to trade. You can also check with the company that you use to trade stocks. If you are unsuccessful in locating that company's stock on either of those exchanges then there is a good chance that it may be a privately held company or listed on an exchange that is located outside of the United States. Privately held companies are companies that do not publically trade its stock on stock exchanges. Although a privately held company may not be selling its stock on a stock exchange it may sell it to investors who inquire about it. If that is the case you should reach out to that company and ask whether it has shares to sell and if it would sell some to you. Most privately held companies have an Investor Relations Department that can answer those questions so that's where you should start.

Generally when an investor wants to buy stock in a company he can't just walk into the NYSE or the NASDAQ to do so. That investor must use the services of a bank or brokerage firm that employs licensed stockbrokers. Those entities are called financial service companies and they require an investor to have an account with them before they will allow their stockbrokers to process a trade for that investor.

Most financial service companies allow its customers to request trades online, which is generally acted upon shortly after the trade is requested. Although there is more to that process than what I am describing, the key point to remember is that in order to trade stocks on a stock exchange you have to go through a licensed stockbroker.

When deciding on which financial service company to use to place your trades you should compare the kind of services that each company offer to its customers. Some financial service companies provide customized research for its customers regarding a company's leadership and the leadership's prior management experience; information about a company's profits and loses; operating expenses; pending lawsuits and management's plans to grow the company.

Some financial service companies even offer online tools, which allow its customers to conduct their own research regarding companies that they are interested in buying stock in. Remember it is always a good idea to consult with a financial advisor before trading stocks so that you make informed decisions about the money that you intend to use to purchase stock.

What to Consider Before Purchasing Stock

Now this may sound silly, but a company that is making money may not always be a good company to invest in. Let's look at a bakery that sells fruit pies, which have become very popular in its local town over the past 2 years. Because of the growing popularity of the pies the owner of that bakery recently began to sell his pies in 5 additional towns, which has resulted in substantially more pies being sold. Because of the increased sales the bakery's owner has found himself in a good, but challenging situation. He cannot keep up with the demand for his pies.

He has storeowners calling him daily demanding that he ship more pies so that they can keep their store shelves filled. They are also threatening to buy pies from another bakery if he doesn't fix his inventory problem quickly. Each day that the stores' shelves are not filled with pies the storeowners are losing money from lost sales. It is understandable why the storeowners would be upset with the baker because it is his failure to adequately prepare for the expansion of his business, which could be viewed by them as mismanagement or poor leadership. The storeowners are not the only ones losing money from the baker's mismanagement or poor leadership. He is to and that's called opportunity cost. He is missing out on an opportunity to gain more revenue from the sale of his pies. The less pies that he ships to the stores the less money he makes in profits.

The baker needed to hire new employees at the time that he decided to expand into those additional towns, but he chose not to. Before the baker decided to expand his sales in those additional towns he operated the factory on one shift, Monday through Friday. His factory has the capacity to operate 24 hours per day 7 days a week. Instead of adding a second or a third shift with more employees working the baker made his current employees work more hours each day, which obviously failed to meet the increased demand for his pies.

As you can image the baker's employees were very tired after their shift and were becoming disgruntle with him. Tired employees increase the risk that they may injure themselves while on the job or that they may mess up the product that they are making. Injured employees mean less people making the product. Moreover, at the time that the baker decided to expand his business he had two delivery trucks, which were in constant need of repair. The drivers of those trucks also became disgruntle with the baker because they too were being forced to work additional hours and drive longer distances each day. Tired drivers lead to bad car accidents and a company being sued because the driver worked for the company. A lawsuit leads to less profit, just saying! If the baker was managing his company wisely and efficiently he would have anticipated the need to hire more employees and the need to acquire additional delivery trucks so that his vision of expanding into additional towns could be successful and profitable.

That kind of forward thinking is required in any business where products are being made or where services are being provided. Lets say that the reason that the baker couldn't afford to hire more people or buy new delivery trucks was because he was spending his profits on other things that were not related to growing his business, such as a new boat to dock at his new lake house. Neither of those purchases contributed to the ongoing growth of the baker's company.

If purchasing new delivery trucks would have been too costly for the baker he could have rented additional delivery trucks until he could have afforded to buy new or used ones. He could have also hired a delivery company to deliver his pies until he could afford to purchase new or used trucks. Those added expenditure is worth the cost because they are contributing to the growth of his business.

Let's say instead of buying the boat and the lake house our baker used part of his profits to purchase new computers for his office in order to organize his business records. Lets also say that he used the rest of his profits to advertise his company and to buy custom made furniture for his newly renovated office. If new furniture and a renovated office can bake pies then the baker made a good decision by purchasing that furniture and renovating his office, but since neither of those things can't bake pies or deliver them to the stores then it is my opinion that he didn't use his profits wisely when it came to those expenditures. The baker has an inventory problem, which is not going to be fixed with new furniture and a renovated office. Moreover, his decision to continually advertise his business when he can't meet the current demand for his pies is not a good use of company's profits either. He should be more focus on keeping his current customers satisfied by ensuring that their store shelves remain full with the pies that they ordered from him.

Sometimes external events or unforeseen events can expose mismanagement or poor leadership in a company.

What effect do you think a worldwide drought will have on our baker's business? It may require him to pay significantly more money for the fruits that he needs to bake his pies, which will increase his monthly expenditures. When faced with unexpected circumstances or events most business owners seek to reduce their operating expenses to cover additional costs. Operating expenses are bills that a business owner pays to keep the company running. They include things such as utilities costs (gas, electric and water); insurance on the building; delivery trucks, equipment; employee payroll; ingredients and supplies. One expense that is generally reduced first is payroll, which requires the laying off or termination of some employees.

When a company is growing or expanding like our bakery and it is faced with an unforeseen event laying off employees in an effort to cut cost to save money may not be a good idea. Fewer employees mean fewer pies and fewer pies mean fewer profits. You should avoid investing in companies that continuingly reduce its payroll costs to cut cost because that could be a sign of mismanagement or poor leadership. Another way companies can reduce their expenses is by raising its prices, shortening the number of hours that its factory is operating or by using lower quality ingredients or material in their product.

When a company chooses to raise the price of its products or discontinue selling some of them that may alienate its customers and force those customers to shop elsewhere for similar items. Our baker have four options to save his business, lay off employees, decrease the hours that the factory is open, raise the prices of his pies or use cheaper ingredients. He chose to use cheaper ingredients to bake his pies. A decision like that may cause an investor to have second thoughts about investing in the baker's company especially if the quality of those ingredients are drastically different from what was previously used to bake those infamous pies.

Most times customers may not immediately notice when a company begin to use cheap ingredients or inferior material in their products, but eventually they will. When the news come out about the lack of quality in a company's product customers generally choose to shop elsewhere for similar items. A business owner who uses cheaper ingredients or material to make his or her product also run the risk of having their customers expose them on social media platforms. Once a business owner's decision to use cheaper ingredients or material is exposed to the world it may be difficult for that company to regain and maintain the loyalty of its customers.

Now paying less for ingredients or material doesn't always mean poor quality. It is possible for a business owner to find a new supplier who will agree to charge him or her less for the same quality of goods, but in our example it is highly unlikely that our baker will find such a supplier. Remember there is a worldwide drought that shrunk the supply of fruit. When demand is so great for a limited number of supplies the price of those items will go up, but when there is a huge supply of an item and little demand for it then the price of that item will generally be low. That is called supply and demand economics.

Let's say that our baker noticed that some of his competitors were going out of business as a result of the higher prices of fruit. He called those businesses and asked if they were willing to sell him their remaining supply of fruit at a discounted rate and to his surprise they said yes.

Luckily for our baker he was able to buy enough fruit at a low price to keep him in business for the rest of the year.

Wise business owners take advantage of the opportunities that are before them or create opportunities, which allows them to put in place creative solutions to succeed just as our baker did when he sought out alternative supply of fruit. It is very important for an investor to research the professional background of the person managing the company that he or she is interested in investing in because not doing so may lead to the lost of his or her investment. You wouldn't want to invest in a company whose owner or top managers have a history of running companies to the ground, so its best to learn as much as you can about them before investing in the company that they are managing or own. Even doing that doesn't guarantee that those individuals won't lose your investment, but it may give you solace to know that you did all that you could to make an informed decision before investing in their company.

With the knowledge and information that you have gained about our baker would you invest in his company, probably not? Why, because he did not, has not and probably will not make good decisions in the future. Since you or anyone else knowing what you know about the baker and how he operates his business won't invest in his company his only other option is to ask his family and friends for the money/investment. Before they say yes, they should first ask to see his business records and conduct their own due diligence. If any investor believes in a company, but not in the owner or management of the company's ability to operate it wisely and efficiently that investor should insist on some pre-conditions before he or she decides to invest in that company. Some of those conditions may include setting aside a certain percentage of the company's profit to handle unexpected events such as increased prices in material and supplies or insist that someone else manages the company.

Not all investors can dictate the terms of their investment in a company, but when it comes to our baker they probably can. Most of the time when the owner of a company or its top managers approach an investor directly about investing in their company the investor is in a better position to dictate the terms and conditions of his or her investment. Recall the golden rule, he who has the gold makes the rules!!!

You may wonder what a shareholder gets in return for buying stock in a company; well apart from an ownership interest in that company they may receive dividends. Dividends are profits that a company made during a certain time period, which are paid to its shareholders for their investment in the company. The more shares of a company's stock that a shareholder owns the more dividends that that shareholder may be entitled to receive. Some companies distribute dividends on a quarterly basis while some do it once a year.

Here's an example on how dividends may be paid to an investor. Let's say that AWESOME COMPANY made $20 million last year after it paid all of its expenses and that it decided to pay its shareholders $1.50 per share in dividends. Let's also say that AWESOME COMPANY had 10 million shares of stock outstanding, which means that 10 million shares of AWESOME COMPANY's stock are owned by various shareholders/investors. Keep in mind that some investors may have purchased multiple shares of stock in

AWESOME COMPANY. For example, a stockholder who owns 300 shares of AWESOME COMPANY's stock at the time that dividends are declared would be entitled to receive $450 in dividends [300 shares x $1.50]. You may think AWESOME COMPANY payment of $1.50 per share is not a lot of money, but it is based upon the size of its profits compared to the number of its shares that are outstanding.

AWESOME COMPANY paying $1.50 per share on 10 million shares of stock totals fifteen million dollars ($15,000,000.00), which leaves AWESOME COMPANY with only $5 million to expand or grow the company. So in that scenario it may be advisable for AWESOME COMPANY to lower the amount of dividend that it has decided to pay its stockholders so that it will have more money to grow and expand its company.

Generally, the more often that a company pays a dividend the more likely that it is to attract new investors. The key to trading stock is to buy low and sell high, but unfortunately there is no way to determine whether you bought a stock too high or too low because they go up and down all the time for a variety of reasons. So look at the stock's long term successive rises and declines for clues regarding the reasons for those peaks and valleys.

Please keep in mind although a company may be consistently paying dividends that there is really no way to know with complete certainty that it is a good company to invest in. For example, companies such as Enron, Lehman Brothers and Tyco International paid dividends, but later filed for bankruptcy. You should Google those companies to learn what lead to their bankruptcy filings. What you discover won't be boring, especially what you read about Tyco! As you read earlier in this book, anything can affect the price of a company's stock. That's why it's always important to consult with a financial advisor before investing in a company directly or via the stock market.

What is Diversification

To diversify means not putting all of your eggs (money) in one basket (industry). You shouldn't buy stocks in companies that are in the same line of business or in the same industry. For example, if a stockholder owned stock in a grocery store and stock in a food processing company and something unforeseen happened both companies might be severely affected by that event. We know that grocery stores make a lot of money selling all kinds of meat and dairy products and that there are companies that process those food items before they reach the grocery store shelves. If you owned stock in companies that are associated with either of those industries when the shortage occurred you would most likely see the price of your stock in those industries decline and possibly see one or more of those companies go out of business.

As you can see from this example, one unexpected event can affect an entire industry. This is why it is highly recommended that stockholders purchase stock in different companies, which are not in the same industry. The rationale behind diversification is the following: if a stockholder owns stock in more than one industry and if an unforeseen event occurs in one of those industries it is presumed that that unforeseen event will not affect the sales in those other industries. A shortage of meat and milk in the meat or grocery industry should not affect or impact the sales in the electronic or airline industries because meat and milk are not used to make electronic products or used in the airline industry.

To demonstrate diversification even further, let's say that you own stock in the toy industry, the airline industry and in the banking industry. Now let's say that people are not having as many children as they use to and because of that parents are not buying as many toys. The decreased sale of toys should not affect the airline or banking industries because whether parents buy more or less toys should not affect how often people fly or when banks loan money to people or business owners.

Lets say that the price of oil increased significantly and people can no longer afford to drive their cars as often as they would like to because its just too expensive to fill up their gas tanks. Which of the following industries do you believe would be *immediately* impacted by a sudden rise in oil prices the airline industry, toy industry or the banking industry? If you said the airline industry then you are correct because airlines use a lot of oil to fly their planes. The immediate spike in oil prices will cause the airline companies to pass on the increased fuel price to its customers through higher ticket prices. Companies love their customers, but they are not going to eat the cost of the higher oil prices for them. I don't know who coined this phrase, it's not personal, but business, but it's true.

It is interesting to note when fuel prices go up people generally purchase fuel-efficient vehicles, which lowers their fuel cost. Higher gas prices also affect automotive manufactures because if people aren't buying larger vehicles then auto manufactures have to start building smaller vehicles to meet the demand for more fuel-efficient cars. No one is going to pay $100 to fill up their large vehicle every week when they can buy a smaller car that will cost less to fill up while travelling the same distance. No wonder auto manufacturers are building electric and hybrid vehicles; doing so makes the auto industry somewhat immune to large increases in oil prices.

As you can see it is very important to know which industry the company that you are interested in investing in is associated with to ensure that your stock portfolio is balanced and diversified. A stock portfolio is a group of stocks that an investor has in their brokerage account. A brokerage account is like a savings account, but that the brokerage account has stocks in it. Having a well-balanced and diversified stock portfolio helps to minimize the losses that you may incur by investing in the stock market.

CONCLUSION

As you have read, deciding on which company to invest in is a very important decision and should not be taken lightly. Some of the key factors to consider prior to trading stocks include understanding the business philosophy of the business owner or top managers of a company; the industry that the company is associated with and the external factors that may affect that company's ability to make money such as food shortages or high oil prices.

Finally, when deciding to divest [sell] yourself from a particular stock in your portfolio you should apply the same principles that I had discussed earlier for buying stock. There is an old saying and unfortunately I don't know who said it. It goes like this: if trading stocks were easy then everyone would be rich. Investing in the stock market is not easy and it is very risky, which is why it is important to seek the advice of a financial advisor before investing your hard earned money in anyone or in the stock market.

PS: May the words in this book inspire you to read other books to further your understanding of the stock market about entrepreneurship! Most importantly, don't invest money that you can't afford to lose!!!

Made in the USA
Coppell, TX
11 February 2021